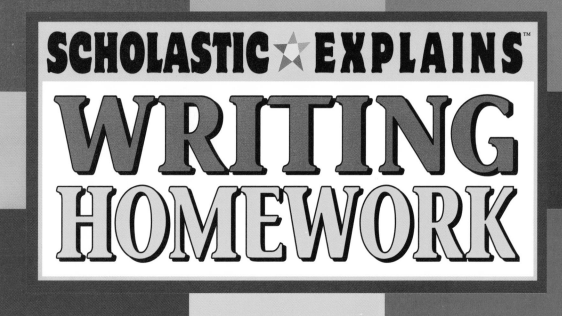

SCHOLASTIC ★ EXPLAINS™
WRITING HOMEWORK

SCHOLASTIC REFERENCE

Produced by Kirchoff/Wohlberg, Inc.
Editorial Director, Mary Jane Martin

CREDITS

Design and Electronic Production: Kirchoff/Wohlberg, Inc.

Illustration: Tom Leonard, 13, 14, 33, 46; Diane Paterson, 17, 62; Diane Blasius, 42; Jared Lee, 46, 47; Arvis Stewart, 48; Liz Callen, 51; Don Madden, 58

Photo Acknowledgments: 4, Art Wolfe/Tony Stone Images; 5, J. Barry O'Rourke/The Stock Market; 6 (top), Paul Barton/The Stock Market; 6 (bottom), Telegraph Colour Library/FPG International; 8, Tom Brakefield/Bruce Coleman, Inc.; 9, Peter Lacz/Peter Arnold, Inc.; 10, Mervyn Rees/Tony Stone Images; 11 (middle), From *Scholastic Children's Dictionary*. Copyright © 1996 by Scholastic, Inc.; 11 (bottom), Laurie Campbell/Tony Stone Images; 12, Richard Hutchings/Photo Researchers; 13, Alan Oddie/PhotoEdit; 14, David Young-Wolff/PhotoEdit; 16, David W. Harp Photography; 18 (top), Copyright © 1945 by E.B. White. Text Copyright renewed © 1973 by E.B. White. Illustrations Copyright renewed © 1973 by Garth Williams. Used by permission of HarperCollins Publishers. This selection may not be re-illustrated; 18 (bottom), New York Times/Archive Photos; 19, Illustrations Copyright renewed © 1980 by Garth Williams. Used by permission of HarperCollins Publishers. No changes may be made to text or art without written permission and are subject to approval from the author/artist or estate thereof; 20/21, From *The Magic School Bus Inside The Human Body* by Joanna Cole, illustrated by Bruce Degen. Illustrations copyright © 1989 by Bruce Degen. Reprinted by permission of Scholastic, Inc. The

Magic School Bus is a registered trademark of Scholastic, Inc.; 22, The Kobal Collection; 23 (top), The Kobal Collection; 23 (bottom), National Museum of American History/Smithsonian Institution; 24, Peter Hince/The Image Bank; 25, Comstock; 26, Blair Seitz/Photo Researchers; 27, Bill Staley/FPG International; 27 (middle right), Stan Osolinski/FPG International; 28, Mary Kate Denny/PhotoEdit; 29 (top), Bill Losh/FPG International; 29 (bottom), Carlos Spaventa/FPG International; 30, Mugshots/The Stock Market; 31, Arthur Tilley/FPG International; 32 (background), Leo DeWys, Inc./DeWys/IFA; 32 (inset), Tom Prettyman/PhotoEdit; 34, Comstock; 35, Index Stock Photography; 36, Stuart Westmorland/Tony Stone Images; 37, T. & D. McCarthy/The Stock Market; 38, John Clark/The Stock Market; 39, Paul Barton/The Stock Market; 40, Art Wolfe/Tony Stone Images; 41, J. Barry O'Rourke/The Stock Market; 43, Comstock; 44, Sanford/International Stock; 45, Stuart Westmorland/Tony Stone Images; 46, David Woods/The Stock Market; 49, E. & P. Bauer/Bruce Coleman, Inc.; 50, Elizabeth Simpson/FPG International; 52, © Eric Sander; 53, Kay Chernush/The Image Bank; 54, Jim Cummins/FPG International; 55, Lori Adamski Peek/Tony Stone Images; 56, Myrleen Ferguson/PhotoEdit; 57, McCarthy/Stock Imagery; 58, The Walk (1943) by Jacob Kainen. Courtesy Mrs. Jacob Kainen; 59, Viviane Moos/The Stock Market; 60, David Young-Wolff/PhotoEdit; 61, Jeff Greenberg/Photo Researchers.

Board of Advisors

Library of Congress Cataloging-in-Publication Data

Scholastic explains writing homework: everything children (and parents) need to survive 2nd and 3rd grades.
p. cm. (The Scholastic explains homework series)
Includes index.

Summary: Presents information on a variety of topics related to learning to write, including various kinds of writing, parts of speech, sentence structure, and punctuation.
ISBN 0-590-39756-7 (hardcover)   ISBN 0-590-39759-1 (pbk.)

1. English language—Composition and exercises—Study and teaching (Primary)—United States—Juvenile literature.
2. Homework—Juvenile literature.
[1. English language—Composition and exercises.   2. English language—Rhetoric.]   I. Scholastic Inc.   II. Title: Writing homework.   III. Series
LB1529,U5S36   1998   372.62'3–dc21   97-44307   CIP   AC

Table of  Contents

Here's How It Works 4

Here's How It Works

A Note to Parents

Your child is hard at work on writing homework. Everything seems fine. But then comes that moan of frustration. This kid needs help.

You may not have thought about nouns and verbs or how to write a book report in a good many years. The homework instructions may be hard to understand, incompletely copied, or just plain missing. That's where this book comes in.

Start with the index or the table of contents. You can look up the assignment subject using the words your child uses (describing word, for example) or the term you remember (adjective). Either way will lead you to the right section. Then just work with your child, reading a definition with examples or following instructions as needed.

To get an overview of the way the writing process is taught in schools these days, read the introduction (pages 6–7) with your child. Not every school uses every step listed there, but your child will know which of the steps he or she has been taught. Knowing what to expect will help you help your child.

At right is a guide to two typical pages from *Scholastic Explains Writing Homework*, with the elements you will find throughout the book.

That's all there is to it. Happy homework!

---

basic definition in language used in the classroom

homework subject

expanded definitions

Describe with Adjectives

ADJECTIVES

An **adjective** is a word that tells more about the noun.

Adjectives may describe number, color, or size.
Adjectives may describe how something looks or sounds.

Adjectives that tell about us
number: two
color: red, yellow, blue
how we look: beautiful
how we sound: noisy
size: big

THE PARROTS

Look at the **two** birds.
The birds are **red**, **blue**, and **yellow**.
The **big** birds are sitting on a tree branch.
It's fun to watch the **beautiful** birds.
Pretend you can hear these **noisy** birds.

40

examples in different kinds of sentences

Callout boxes

examples in different kinds of sentences

find topics in ABC order at the end of the book, on page 64

words teachers use, highlighted and explained

ideas to use in the homework assignment

Index (sample page)

Sample page (page 41)

Adjectives may describe how something tastes, feels, or smells.

DELICIOUS!

Dan likes the **delicious** ice cream.
The **cold** ice cream is covered with chocolate.
The **gooey** chocolate drips on Dan's hand.
The chocolate smells **sweet**.

Adjectives that tell about the ice cream
how it tastes: delicious
how it feels: cold

Adjectives that tell about the chocolate
how it feels: gooey
how it smells: sweet

EXTRA HELP

Here are some adjectives you may want to use.

red	beautiful	one	round	noisy
yellow	pretty	two	square	quiet
blue	bright	three	flat	loud
green	lovely	four	big	soft
orange	cute	many	huge	hard
black	adorable	few	little	tasty
white	great	some	short	sour
pink	nice	several	long	sweet

NOTE
Adjectives are also called **describing words**.

41

Introduction

THE WRITING PROCESS

Writing is something you do in steps. These steps are often called the Writing Process. Here are some steps to help you when you write.

PREWRITE

- Choose your **topic**, the subject you are going to write about.
- **Brainstorm** ideas by talking about them with friends. *(See pages 8–9 for help.)*
- Make these decisions:

  What will my **role** be? (Storyteller? Reviewer?)

  Who is my **audience**? (My class? Aunt Cary?)

  In what **form** will I write? (A report? A postcard?) *(See pages 12–29 for help.)*

  What is my **purpose** for writing? (To explain something? To put on a play?)

DRAFT

Use the topic, the ideas, and the decisions you made in **Prewrite** for your first draft. Writing down your ideas for the first time is called **writing a first draft**.

REVISE

Read your first draft and think about how you can make it better. This checklist can help you.

Revision Checklist

Role	Is it clear who is telling the story?
	Is the same person telling the whole story?
Audience	Have I given enough information?
	Is my writing interesting?
	Will my audience understand my purpose for writing?
Form	Is there a clear beginning, middle, and end to my writing?
	Have I chosen the best form for my purpose?
Topic	Is my topic clear?
	Have I included the important ideas about my topic?

After you have read your work, ask someone else to read it. Use your own ideas and what your reader says when you **revise** your work.

PROOFREAD

When you have made your revisions, **proofread** your work. You may want to use this checklist.

Proofreading Marks

⬭	check spelling
⧸B	lower case
b̲̲	capital letter
∧	add
∽→	move
ℓ	cross out
⌗	indent paragraph

Proofreading Checklist

- Have I spelled every word correctly?
- Have I written complete sentences? (*See pages 56–57 for help.*)
- Do all my sentences begin with a capital letter and end with a punctuation mark? (*See pages 54–55 and 58–59 for help.*)
- Do the subjects of my sentences agree with the verbs? (*See pages 54–57 for help.*)
- Have I used commas and other punctuation marks correctly? (*See pages 54–55, 58–59, and 60–61 for help.*)
- Did I indent paragraphs?
- Is my handwriting neat and easy to read? (*See pages 62–63 for help.*)

PUBLISH

You **publish** your work by sharing it with others. Here are some ways to do that.

- Draw pictures and turn your work into a book that others can read.
- Read your work aloud to someone.
- Put your work on a computer and print out copies for your friends and family.

Brainstorm!

GRAPHIC ORGANIZERS FOR WRITING

A **graphic organizer** is a kind of drawing, a word map you make to show how you are putting your ideas together. Before you set up your organizer, you can list all the information you have about your topic. Then use your graphic organizer to show how your ideas are related.

FACTS ABOUT PORCUPINES

Appearance
- covered with quills
- spiny
- look like cactuses

Habitat
- deep, cool forests
- sit in trees
- live in northern areas of North America

Behavior
- come out at night
- do not hibernate in winter
- eat only plants

Self-Defense
- raise quills when threatened
- don't usually attack first
- can lash out with tail

How They Live
sit in trees
do not hibernate in winter

How They Feed
eat only plants
look for food at night

The Life of the Porcupine

How They Act
do not attack first
do not shoot quills

How They Protect Themselves
back into enemies
raise quills when threatened

HIP, HIP, HIPPOS

A **word map** like this can help you brainstorm words to include in your writing. When you write your draft, you can decide which words to use.

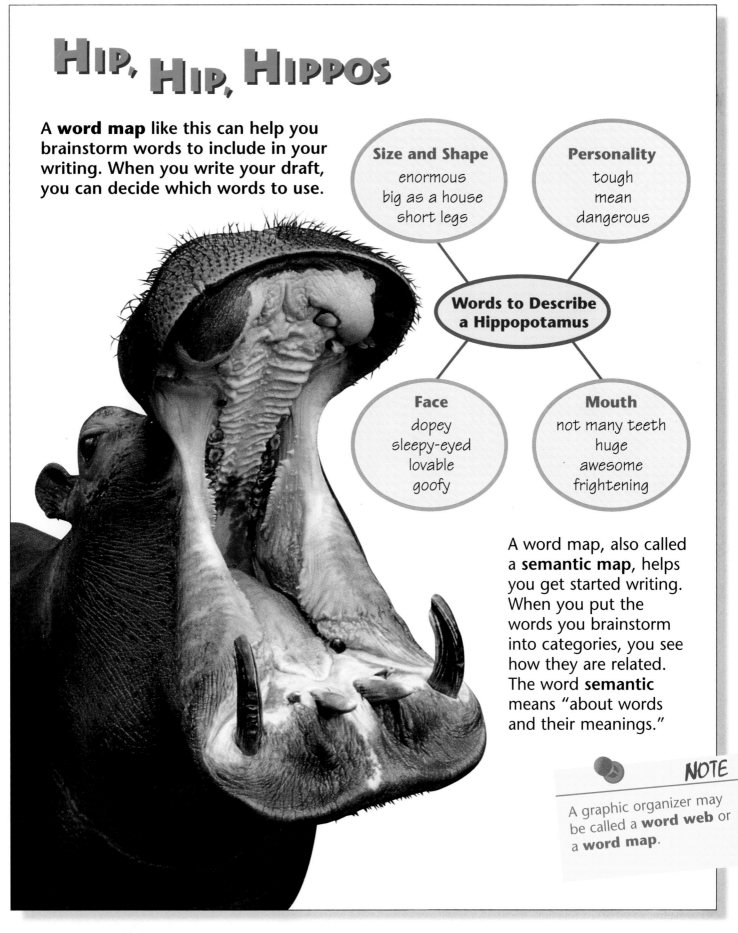

Size and Shape
enormous
big as a house
short legs

Personality
tough
mean
dangerous

Words to Describe a Hippopotamus

Face
dopey
sleepy-eyed
lovable
goofy

Mouth
not many teeth
huge
awesome
frightening

A word map, also called a **semantic map**, helps you get started writing. When you put the words you brainstorm into categories, you see how they are related. The word **semantic** means "about words and their meanings."

NOTE

A graphic organizer may be called a **word web** or a **word map**.

Looking It Up

ALPHABETICAL ORDER

When you write, you often need to look up the spelling of a word in the dictionary. Sometimes you will want to use an encyclopedia to find out more about a topic. Dictionaries and encyclopedias are in **alphabetical order**. This is also called **ABC order**.

Looking for Swans

Here's how to find *swan* in the dictionary.

First, look at the **guide words** at the top of the dictionary pages. The guide words tell you the first and last words on each page. Find the words that begin with *s*. Look at the second and third letters of the two guide words. Find the page where the word *swan* comes *between* the two guide words in alphabetical order. You will find *swan* on that page.

When you are trying to look up a word among a lot of words that start with the same letter, look at the second letter. For instance, *sand* would be listed before *sit*. Sometimes several words begin with the same two or three letters. The words *swamp* and *swan* both begin with *swa*. To find *swan* in ABC order, you need to look at the fourth letter.

Nuthatch
Oriole
Ovenbird
Parrot
Peacock
Pigeon
Quail
Quetzal
Raven
Robin
Sandpiper
Sparrow
Swan
Teal
Thrush ▶
Turkey
Upland Plover
Vireo
Vulture
Warbler
Whippoorwill
Woodpecker
Wren
Xantus
Yellowthroat
Zone-tailed Hawk

suspend ▶ swap

3. (suh-spekt) *verb* To have doubts about; to distrust. *She said she really wants to help, but I suspect her sincerity.*
4. (suhss-pekt) *noun* Someone thought to be responsible for a crime.
▷ *verb* **suspecting, suspected**

sus·pend (suh-spend) *verb*
1. To attach something to a support so that it hangs downward. *We suspended the banner from the gym ceiling.*
2. To keep from falling as if attached from above. *The hummingbird was suspended over the flower.*
3. To stop something for a short time. *Work was suspended for the holidays.*
4. To punish someone by stopping the person from taking part in an activity for a short while. *Sophie was suspended from school for a week.*
▷ *verb* **suspending, suspended** ▷ *noun* **suspension**

sus·pend·ers (suh-spen-durz) *noun, plural* A pair of elastic straps worn over the shoulders and attached to pants or a skirt to hold up the garment.

sus·pense (suh-spenss) *noun* An anxious and uncertain feeling caused by having to wait to see what happens. *We were all in suspense as we waited to learn the winners of the contest.*

sus·pen·sion bridge (suh-spen-shuhn) *noun* A bridge hung from cables or chains strung from towers.

sus·pi·cion (suh-spish-uhn) *noun*
1. A thought, based more on feeling than on fact, that something is wrong or bad.
2. If you are **under suspicion**, people think that you may have done something wrong.

sus·pi·cious (suh-spish-uhss) *adjective*
1. If you feel **suspicious**, you think that something is wrong or bad, but you have little or no proof to back up your feelings.
2. If you think that someone seems or looks **suspicious**, you have a feeling that the person has done something wrong and cannot be believed or trusted.

sus·tain (suh-stayn) *verb*
1. To keep something going. *Jeremy sustained a conversation with his cousin for over two hours.*
2. If something **sustains** you, it gives you the energy and strength to keep going. *The hot soup sustained the walkers for miles.*
3. To suffer something. *Tracey sustained some nasty bruises.*
▷ *verb* **sustaining, sustained**

swag·ger (swa-) *verb* To walk or act in a bold, concei... ly swaggered down the hall, trying t... ...nt. ▷ **swaggering, swaggered** ▷

swal·low (swahl-oh)
1. *verb* To make food or drink travel down from your mouth to your stomach. ▷ *noun* **swallow**
2. *verb* To cause to disappear as if by swallowing. *The raging flood swallowed the house.*
3. *verb* To keep back. *I swallowed my pride.*
4. *noun* A migrating bird with long wings and a forked tail.
5. *verb* (informal) To accept or believe without question. *The story is too wild to swallow.*
▷ *verb* **swallowing, swallowed**

swallow

swamp (swahmp)
1. *noun* An area of wet, spongy ground; a marsh. ▷ *adjective* **swampy**
2. *verb* To fill with or sink in water. *The stormy seas swamped the boat.*
3. *verb* To overwhelm. *I am swamped with homework.*
▷ *verb* **swamping, swamped**

swan (swahn) *noun* A large water bird with white feathers, webbed feet, and a long, graceful neck. *The picture shows a female swan with her young.*

swan and cygnets

S

swank·y (swang-kee) *adjective* (informal) Very elegant or stylish, as in *a swanky restaurant.*

swap (swahp) *verb* (informal) To trade or exchange one thing for another. *I'll swap you my CD for a video game.* ▷ **swapping, swapped** ▷ *noun* **swap**

541

How Do You Do That?

WRITE A HOW-TO PIECE

A **how-to piece** tells how to do something in step-by-step sequence.

Recipes are how-to pieces people use every day.

Recipes are step-by-step directions for how to make something.

The steps are often numbered to show the right order.

BROWNIES

1. Preheat oven to 350° F.
2. Lightly grease a 9-inch x 12-inch baking pan.
3. Combine:
   brownie mix
   1/2 cup water
   1/2 cup vegetable oil
   1 egg
   1/2 cup chopped nuts
4. Mix well.
5. Spread in greased baking pan.
6. Bake for 30–33 minutes.
7. Let cool before cutting.

12

Blowing Bubbles

Here are six steps to follow when you write a how-to piece.

1. Choose something you have done many times.
2. Think about how you do it.
3. Make a list of all the things you do.
4. Review your list to make sure you haven't left anything out.
5. Rewrite your list into numbered steps.
6. See if a friend can follow the steps.

EXTRA HELP

When you write a how-to, start directions with a verb that commands.

Get	Find	Dig
Cut	Shake	Bake
Color	Add	Check

(See pages 38–39 for more help.)

How to Blow Bubbles

1. Make up the bubble mixture in a dish pan.
   - 1 quart water
   - 8 tablespoons dish detergent
   - 1 tablespoon glycerin (from drugstore)
2. Find things to use for bubble wands.
3. Dip a wand in the bubble mixture.
4. Wave the wand or blow through it to make bubbles.

NOTE

How-to pieces may also be called **directions** or **step-by-step instructions**.

A Book You Will Like

A **book report** should include the following things:

- the **title** of the book,
- the name of the **author** and the **illustrator**,
- a **summary** of the story,
- a **comparison** with another book you have read,
- reasons why you would or would not recommend the book to your friends.

A Funny Book

The Shrinking of Treehorn
Written by Florence Parry Heide
Illustrated by Edward Gorey

<table>
<tr><td>

This book is about a boy named Treehorn who lives with his mother and father in a place that seems like England.

</td><td>

Here are the title and names of the author and the illustrator.

</td></tr>
</table>

This book is about a boy named Treehorn who lives with his mother and father in a place that seems like England. — *This tells about the setting and the characters.*

The problem in the story is that Treehorn is shrinking. At first, his parents don't believe him. But he keeps getting smaller and smaller. He gets so small that his friends, the school bus driver, and his teacher don't recognize him right away.

When he gets so small that he can walk under his bed, he finds a game he had been playing. He never finished the game because his mother had called him to dinner. The game was called THE BIG GAME FOR KIDS TO GROW ON. He starts to play the game. When he does, he gets bigger until he is his regular size again.

This summary of the story tells about the problem and solving the problem.

This book is like George Shrinks, because a boy shrinks in that book, too.

The book is compared to another book here.

This is a very funny book. I think other kids will enjoy it, too.

The writer recommends the book here.

EXTRA HELP

Making a book map can help you write a book summary.

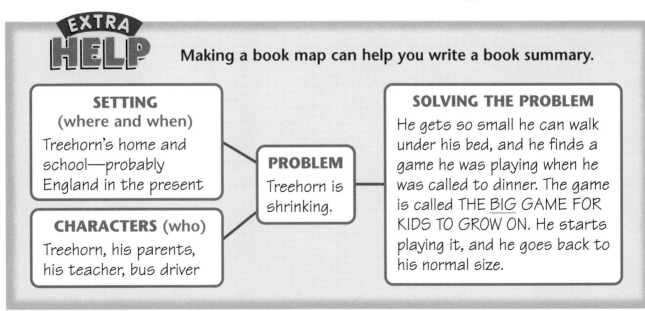

SETTING
(where and when)
Treehorn's home and school—probably England in the present

CHARACTERS (who)
Treehorn, his parents, his teacher, bus driver

PROBLEM
Treehorn is shrinking.

SOLVING THE PROBLEM
He gets so small he can walk under his bed, and he finds a game he was playing when he was called to dinner. The game is called THE BIG GAME FOR KIDS TO GROW ON. He starts playing it, and he goes back to his normal size.

Find Out About It, Then Write!

WRITE AN ARTICLE

Articles

- are nonfiction.
- tell something about a **subject**.
- give **information** that is based on facts.

To write an article, you should first choose a **subject**. Learn everything you can about it, and make a list of the facts you think you could use in a story.

Llamas

Llamas are curious about everything.

Llamas are good at protecting sheep. They scare away coyotes.

They give an alarm call. Then they chase an animal that might attack.

Sometimes they even kick or paw at it.

Llamas are not afraid of some dangerous animals. Bears don't scare them.

Llamas make good pack animals for hikers.

Think about the information you have gathered. How could you use it in a story? Then make an outline or map of the story.

> ### Story Map
>
> **Characters**
> A family—mother, father, and child—and a llama
> **Setting**
> The mountains where the family is hiking and camping out
> **Problem**
> On the trail they meet a bear.
> **Solving the Problem**
> The llama stares at the bear, and the bear goes away.

When you have planned out your story, you're ready to write.

Llamas on the Trail

We were hiking in the mountains. Dad was up ahead, leading the llama that was carrying our camping stuff. Suddenly, Dad stopped. Mom and I stopped, too. I didn't know what was happening. Dad was standing perfectly still, looking at something beside the trail. The llama was looking at it, too, with a curious, interested look on its face. I looked where they were looking, and that's when I saw it. A bear!

I held my breath. Would the bear attack our llama? Would the bear attack us? Everything was quiet. The bear stared at our llama. Our llama stared at the bear. Dad, Mom, and I could hear our hearts thumping. Then the bear made a little snorting sound, turned, and walked away.

Our llama and the bear had had a staring contest, and our llama won!

You can get information for an informational story from

- reading an encyclopedia.
- reading books and magazine articles.
- watching a TV show.
- observing something for yourself.

The Real Lives of Real People

WRITE A BIOGRAPHY

A **biography** is the story of a real person's life. A biography doesn't have to tell about a person's whole life, but what it tells must be true. A **short biography** might describe just a few important events in someone's life.

E. B. White and *Stuart Little*

E. B. White was born on July 11, 1899, in Mount Vernon, New York. "E. B." stands for Elwyn Brooks. He was the youngest child in a large family. He began writing when he was very young.

He graduated from Cornell University in 1921 and went to work on a magazine in New York. One day in the 1920s, he took a train from New York City to the Shenandoah Valley in Virginia just to walk around and enjoy a beautiful spring day. On his way back to New York, he fell asleep on the train and had a dream about "a small character who had the features of a mouse," and "was nicely dressed."

White began making up stories about the little mouse character for his nieces and nephews. Over the years, he saved the stories and created more. Finally they became the book Stuart Little, which was published in 1945—almost twenty years after he first dreamed about the mouse.

This part of E. B. White's biography tells

- when he was born.
- where he was born.
- how he started out as a writer.
- how he came to write books for children.

The Best-Known Book

E. B. White and
Charlotte's Web

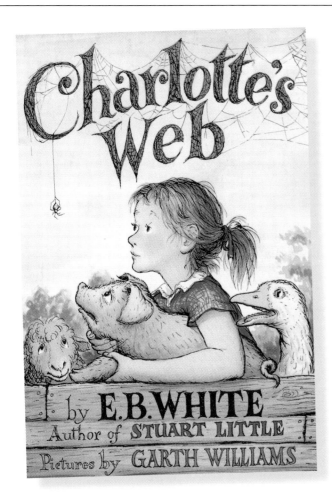

Later, E. B. White moved to a farm in Maine where he raised animals, including pigs. He wrote his second children's book, Charlotte's Web, when he was living on the farm. White had decided to write a children's book about animals. One day he was feeding a pig, and it made him sad to think that the pig would have to die. Then he saw a big gray spider. That gave him an idea for a way to write a story about a pig whose life was saved. It took him three years to write the book, Charlotte's Web, which was published in 1952. It is his best-known book.

This part of E. B. White's biography tells

- what gave him the idea for *Charlotte's Web*.
- when *Charlotte's Web* was written and published.

You can find information to help you write a biography

- by reading letters the person wrote.
- by reading diaries or memoirs the person wrote.
- by seeing photographs of the person.
- by talking to the person.
- by reading about the person in an encyclopedia.
- by reading books about the person.
- by seeing a movie or TV show about the person.

NOTE

A biography is always written by another person. An **autobiography** is written by the person it is about.

What a Character!

WRITE ABOUT A STORY CHARACTER

To understand a story, you need to understand the characters in a story—what they are thinking, how they feel, and why they do the things they do. You learn about **story characters** through

- **what the author says about them.**
- **what other characters say about them.**
- **what the characters themselves say and do.**
- **what the illustrator shows about them.**

When you write about a character, look in the story for these clues. You may want to create a **character map.**

MY FAVORITE CARNIVORE

MS. FRIZZLE

What the author says

"Ms. Frizzle was the strangest teacher in the school."

What other characters say

"Is she for real?"

"She must buy her clothes in outer space."

What the illustrator shows

She has messy red hair.

Her clothes, shoes, and earrings match the science topic she is teaching.

What the character says and does

"Children, prepare for landing."

She takes her class on weird field trips in a magic school bus.

She makes the bus shrink so that Arnold will swallow it with his Cheesie-Weesies and the class can explore inside the human body.

You can use your character map
to write about the character.

THE FRIZ

Ms. Frizzle is the strangest teacher in
school. She wears strange dresses and
strange shoes. But the strangest thing
about her is the way she teaches
science. When the class was studying
the human body, she actually took them on
a field trip inside Arnold, one of the kids in the class.

They were going to the science museum in the magic
school bus. They had lunch at a park, and when it was time
to go, Arnold didn't get back on the bus. He was
daydreaming and eating Cheesie-Weesies. Instead
of going to the museum, Ms. Frizzle made the bus so
small that Arnold swallowed it with his Cheesie-
Weesies, and the whole class ended up in Arnold's
digestive system. When a white blood cell started chasing
the bus, Ms. Frizzle made everybody get out and grab onto
a red blood cell! All the time she is doing these weird things,
she acts as if nothing unusual is happening!

LOOK! WHEN THE
RED BLOOD CELLS
PICK UP OXYGEN, THEY
TURN <u>BRIGHT</u> <u>RED</u>.

EXTRA HELP

When you write about a story character

- remember what the author and the other characters say
  about your character, and try to use some of the same words.
- remember what the character looks like in the pictures.
- give an example of something the character does.
- add your own thoughts about the character.
- think about how the character feels.
- try to figure out why the character acts the way she does.

It's Worth the Cost of a Ticket

WRITE A REVIEW

A review of a movie or TV show gives the reviewer's opinion of it.

A review

- tells what the movie or show is about without giving away the ending.
- tells what was good about the movie.
- tells what could have been better.

People read reviews of movies and TV shows to help them decide what they want to see. Keep that in mind when you are writing about a movie. Don't tell the whole story. Just help the reader decide if the movie is worth going to see or if it is a waste of time.

The Wizard of Oz

The Wizard of Oz is a very old movie. The special effects in this movie aren't like special effects today. It doesn't look real at all when the tornado picks the house up off the ground. But that's nice, in a way, because it makes it funny and not scary. You know nobody is getting hurt.

This movie has a lot of neat things. I like the way it starts out in black and white and changes to color when Dorothy lands in Oz.

I also like how Elvira Gulch and the Wicked Witch of the West are the same person. The farm hands are the same people as the Scarecrow, the Tin Man, and the Cowardly Lion, too.

I think anyone who hasn't already seen The Wizard of Oz should see it. It's fun, and it's neat to see a movie your parents and your grandparents saw when they were kids.

This movie review tells
- some things that might be better if the movie were newer.
- things the reviewer liked.
- why someone would want to see the movie.

Let's Have a Talk

WRITE A DIALOGUE

Dialogue is what the characters in a play or a story say.

In the dialogue for a play, the speaker's tag tells who is speaking.

The speaker's tag looks like this: **Ingrid:**

It is followed by exactly what the speaker says.

Akimi

Stewart

Scottie

Ingrid

Ingrid: I'm so tired of standing here.

Scottie: I think *my* arm's asleep.

Akimi: I need to go to the bathroom.

Stewart: I can't believe *you* said that!

24

A Great Game

In a story, what the characters say is set off by **quotation marks**.

"You played a great game today, little brother," said Greg.

"But I still didn't beat you," said Windell.

"Once you start beating me," laughed Greg, "I might not want to play with you anymore."

Always put **commas, periods, and end punctuation** before the quotation marks. Start each quotation with a **capital letter**.

EXTRA HELP

There are many words you can use to tell how someone said something.

"Mirror, mirror on the wall, who's the fairest of them all?" **asked** the Queen.

"I wish I could walk on land," **sighed** the Little Mermaid.

"Everyone stay on the bus!" **shouted** the Friz.

"Some pig!" **whispered** Mr. Zuckerman.

"And don't talk to strangers," Red Riding Hood's mother **warned**.

Any Mail for Me?

WRITE A LETTER

A letter that you write to say thank you, or just to say hello, is a **friendly letter**.

A friendly letter has four important parts: a **greeting**, the **body**, the **closing**, and the **signature**. Some friendly letters include a **heading** with the writer's address and the date.

Lisa Drew
84 Harmony Lane
Sunnyside, PA 18555

Ms. Diane Drew
210 Ridge Drive
Santa Monica, CA 90400

84 Harmony Lane
Sunnyside, PA 18555

January 8, 1998

Dear Aunt Di,

Thanks for the great birthday present. How did you know I wanted a watch like that? I put it on the minute I got it, and I've worn it every day since.

I hope to see you soon.

Love,
Lisa

The heading goes here.

The date goes here.

This is the greeting.

The body of the letter begins here

and ends here.

This is the closing and the signature.

Greetings from Nick

Writing a **postcard** is like writing a friendly letter. There should be a greeting, a body, a closing, and a signature. You can leave out the date. It's on the postmark.

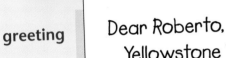

greeting

Dear Roberto,
   Yellowstone Park is some amazing place.

body

We saw a moose yesterday. I hope to see a bear next.
   Wish you were here.

closing

   Your best friend,

signature

Nick Bridger

Roberto Fuentes
711 West 79th St.
New York, NY 10024

EXTRA HELP

Here are some other **closings** you might like to use:

Yours truly,	Your friend,	Best regards,
Sincerely yours,	Sincerely,	Best wishes,
Very truly yours,	Your pen pal,	Love and kisses,

Remember to put a **comma** after the greeting and the closing.

NOTE

If the closing is more than one word, only the first word is capitalized.

Like a Song

A **poem** is a piece of writing set out in short lines, often with a noticeable rhythm and some words that rhyme. Many poems are written to help the reader or listener share an experience or feel a strong emotion. In a poem, words are often chosen for their sounds as well as their meanings.

In these poems, lines 2 and 4 rhyme. Write a poem that rhymes like a poem you know.

The Little Nut Tree

I had a little nut tree.
Nothing would it bear,
But a silver nutmeg,
And a golden pear.

The Little Puppy

I had a little puppy.
I took him for a walk.
He barked to tell me something.
I wish that he could talk.

Follow a Pattern

Another way to write a poem is to follow a format or **pattern**. When you use a format, the poem you create may not rhyme. Poems don't need to rhyme.

Here's a format to try.

Line 1: Tell what the subject of your poem is.

Line 2: Write three adjectives that describe your subject. (*See pages 40–41 and 42–43 for help.*)

Line 3: Write four *-ing* words that tell things your subject does.

Line 4: Write three nouns that describe your subject. (*See pages 30–31 and 32–33 for help.*)

Line 5: Tell the subject again.

Here are two poems that use the pattern.

My dog Ruff
Shaggy, lovable, loyal
Jumping, slobbering, panting, fetching
Partner, helper, friend
My dog Ruff

Kittens
Tiny, furry, soft
Sleeping, meowing, playing, growing
Love, life, fun
Kittens

EXTRA HELP

Some rhyming words are spelled alike.		Some aren't.	
mouse—house	pickle—tickle	laugh—giraffe	he—sea
log—frog	nurse—purse	tough—stuff	her—purr
cat—hat	moose—goose	cough—off	kite—sight
fun—sun	how—now	world—twirled	word—bird
walk—talk	name—game	paws—cause	socks—fox

Name That Noun!

NOUNS

A **noun** is a word that names a person, a place, or a thing.

person	place	thing
boy	school	pencil
student	classroom	book
son	home	sweater
brother	kitchen	table

Nouns can also name feelings and ideas.

feelings	ideas or thoughts
happiness	work
anger	freedom
excitement	fun
hunger	success

Nouns that are names of particular people, places, and things are called **proper nouns**. They begin with **capital letters**.

Nouns that do not name particular people, places, or things are called **common nouns**. They do not begin with capital letters.

A ZIPPY Floater

This is **Chandra Brown**. She is in the pool at **Water Park** in **Silver City**, **Utah**. Chandra is using a **Zippy Floater**.

These are **proper nouns**

person	Chandra Brown
place	Water Park Silver City Utah
thing	Zippy Floater

EXTRA HELP

Here are some **common nouns**.

person	place	thing
artist	planet	computer
doctor	mall	toy
mom	country	tent
brother	city	bicycle
friend	forest	flower
dad	bakery	book

Here are some **proper nouns**.

person	place	thing
David	France	X ray
Ana Gomez	Mars	Statue of Liberty
George Washington	Dallas, Texas	the Liberty Bell

NOTE

A **common noun** may also be called a **regular noun**.

Runner's or Runners'?

SINGULAR, PLURAL, AND POSSESSIVE NOUNS

A **singular noun** is a word that names one person, place, or thing.

A **plural noun** is a word that names more than one person, place, or thing.

For most singular nouns, add -s to make the plural.

singular	plural
runner	runners
prize	prizes
avenue	avenues

The Great Race

My dad is a **runner** in this race.
The **runners** are ready to go.
I hope he wins a **prize**.
There are three **prizes**.

A **possessive noun** shows who owns something.

You can make a singular noun into a possessive noun by adding an **apostrophe** and an **s**.

My **dad's** new shoes help him run.
    The **'s** shows that my dad owns the shoes.

Erin's mom is running, too.
    The **'s** shows that the mom belongs to Erin.

You can make a plural noun into a possessive plural by adding an apostrophe after the **s**.

All the **runners'** shoes are muddy.
    The **'** shows that the shoes belong to a group of runners.

Always add **'s** to a **singular noun** even when it ends with **s**.

Running is **Jonas's** favorite sport.
He is his **class's** best runner.

Brushes, Berries, and Geese

Here are some other ways to change singular nouns to plural nouns.

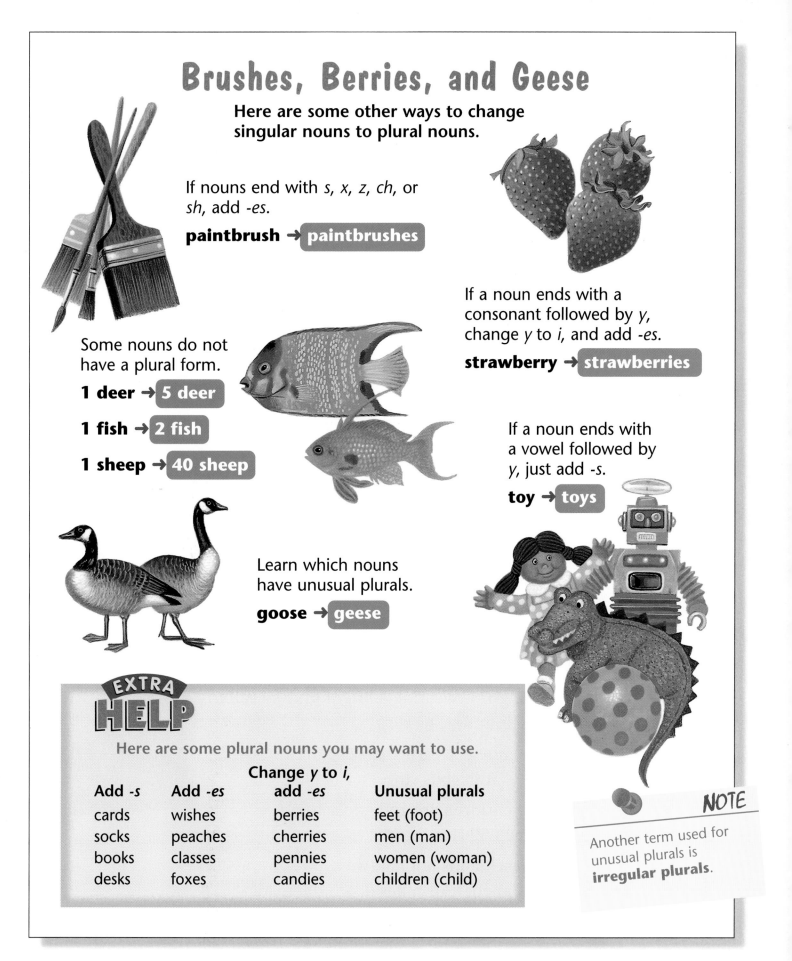

If nouns end with *s*, *x*, *z*, *ch*, or *sh*, add -*es*.

paintbrush → **paintbrushes**

Some nouns do not have a plural form.

1 deer → **5 deer**

1 fish → **2 fish**

1 sheep → **40 sheep**

If a noun ends with a consonant followed by *y*, change *y* to *i*, and add -*es*.

strawberry → **strawberries**

If a noun ends with a vowel followed by *y*, just add -*s*.

toy → **toys**

Learn which nouns have unusual plurals.

goose → **geese**

EXTRA HELP

Here are some plural nouns you may want to use.

Add -s	Add -es	Change y to i, add -es	Unusual plurals
cards	wishes	berries	feet (foot)
socks	peaches	cherries	men (man)
books	classes	pennies	women (woman)
desks	foxes	candies	children (child)

NOTE

Another term used for unusual plurals is **irregular plurals**.

33

Putting Pronouns in Their Place

PRONOUNS

A noun is a word that names a person, a place, or a thing.
A **pronoun** is a word that can take the place of a noun.

At the Bus Stop

One **girl** is wearing a bright blue sweater.
She is at the bus stop.

One **boy** is wearing a baseball cap.
He is at the bus stop.

The **children** are going to school.
They will ride the bus.

The **school** is not far away.
It is about four miles down the road.

noun	pronoun
boy	he
girl	she
children	they
school	it

A **pronoun** can also take the place of a **proper noun**.

The **personal pronouns** I, you, we, or they can take the place of a person's name.

Jill's FUNNY Story

"I like your story," said **Sam**.

Sam says **I** when he talks about himself.

"**You** wrote a good story," Cary said to **Jill**.

Cary says **you** when he talks directly to someone.

"**We** think your story is funny," said **Cary and Sam**.

Cary and Sam say **we** when they talk about themselves.

"When Joann and Lee read it, **they** will like it, too," said Jill.

Jill uses **they** when she talks about other people.

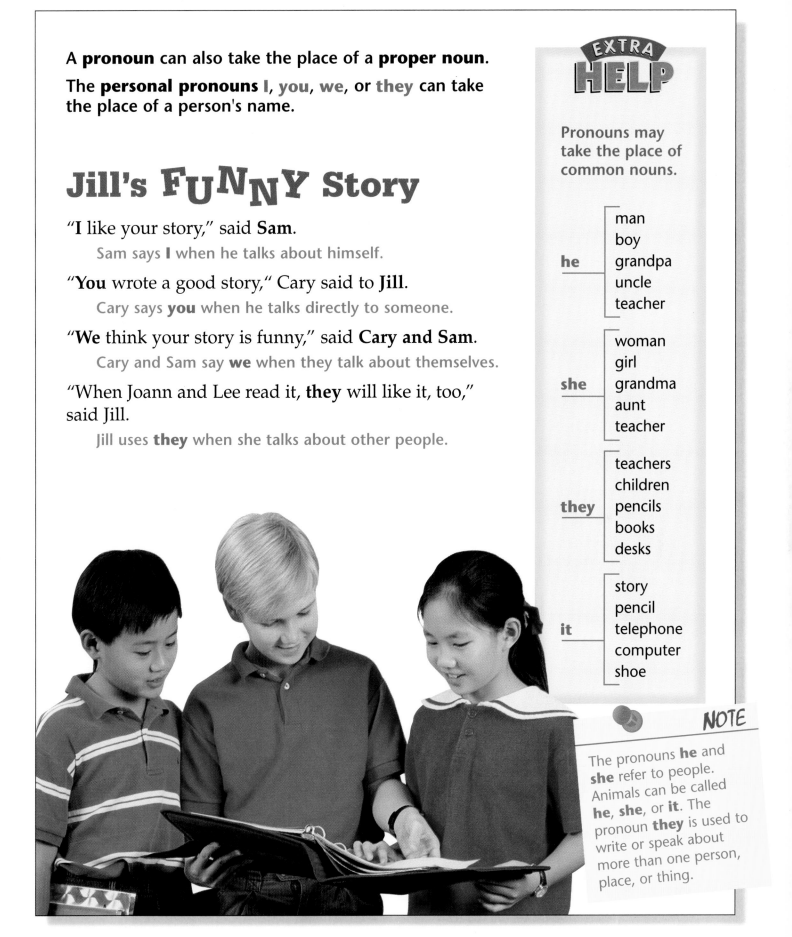

35

I See You, You See Me

OBJECT AND POSSESSIVE PRONOUNS

A **pronoun** is a word that can take the place of a noun.

Some pronouns can be the subject of a sentence. They are called subject pronouns. **I** and **we**, **he**, **she**, and **they** are **subject pronouns**. (*See pages 56–57 for help.*)

Other pronouns can be the object of a sentence or a phrase. **Me** and **us**, **him**, **her**, and **them** are **object pronouns**.

Possessive pronouns take the place of possessive nouns. **My** and **our**, **his**, **her**, and **their** are possessive pronouns.

Two Seals

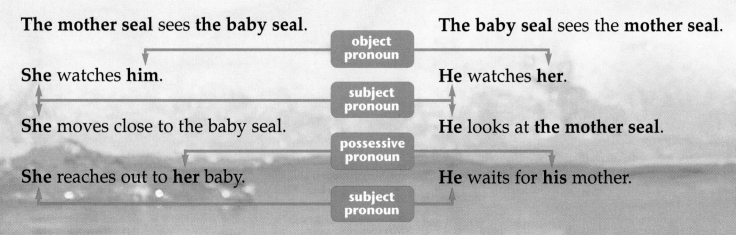

The mother seal sees **the baby seal**.	object pronoun	**The baby seal** sees the **mother seal**.
She watches **him**.	subject pronoun	**He** watches **her**.
She moves close to the baby seal.	possessive pronoun	**He** looks at **the mother seal**.
She reaches out to **her** baby.	subject pronoun	**He** waits for **his** mother.

Tyler's Riddle

Tyler just asked a **riddle**.
Who will get to answer **it**?

Jared thinks **he** knows.
Shall I call on **him**?

Gabby thinks **she** knows.
Shall I call on **her**?

Usha and **Kim** think **they** know.
Shall I call on **them**?

Gabby says, "**I** know.
Call on **me**."

Tyler wonders who can answer
his riddle.

EXTRA HELP

Pronouns

Subjects	Objects	Possessives
I	me	my, mine
you	you	your, yours
she	her	her, hers
he	him	his
it	it	its
we	us	our, ours
they	them	their, theirs

What barks
and bites but
isn't a dog?

(A seal)

Tell It with a Verb

VERBS

A **verb** is a word that tells about an action.

Some verbs tell about actions that are happening now. These verbs are in the **present tense**.

DUCKS

The ducks **swim**.

Verbs that tell what the ducks do	
swim	float
glide	paddle
follow	lead

Some verbs are called **being** verbs. **Am**, **is**, **are**, **was**, and **were** are being verbs.

One duck **is** ahead of all the rest.

Add **-s** to a verb to tell what one person, animal, or thing does.

swim–swims	paddle–paddles
One duck swims.	One duck paddles.
float–floats	follow–follows
One duck floats.	One duck follows.
glide–glides	lead–leads
One duck glides.	One duck leads.

(See pages 56–57 for help.)

Some verbs name actions that happened in the past.

These verbs are in the **past tense**.

> Yesterday Tracy **skated** in the park.
>
> Her friends **went** with her.
>
> Tracy's dog **pulled** her.
>
> Her friends **laughed** when they **saw** what he **did**.

Add **-ed** to most verbs to show that an action happened in the past. These are regular verbs.	Some verbs change to show that an action happened in the past. These are irregular verbs.
now in the past pull pulled laugh laughed	now in the past go went do did see saw

Describe with Adjectives

ADJECTIVES

An **adjective** is a word that tells more about the noun.

Adjectives may describe number, color, or size.
Adjectives may describe how something looks or sounds.

Adjectives that tell about us
number: two
color: red, yellow, blue
how we look: beautiful
how we sound: noisy
size: big

THE PARROTS

Look at the **two** birds.
The birds are **red, blue**, and **yellow**.
The **big** birds are sitting on a tree branch.
It's fun to watch the **beautiful** birds.
Pretend you can hear these **noisy** birds.

Adjectives may describe how something tastes, feels, or smells.

DELICIOUS!

Dan likes the **delicious** ice cream.

The **cold** ice cream is covered with chocolate.

The **gooey** chocolate drips on Dan's hand.

The chocolate smells **sweet**.

> **Adjectives that tell about the ice cream**
>
> **how it tastes:** delicious
> **how it feels:** cold
>
> **Adjectives that tell about the chocolate**
>
> **how it feels:** gooey
> **how it smells:** sweet

EXTRA HELP

Here are some adjectives you may want to use.

red	beautiful	one	round	noisy
yellow	pretty	two	square	quiet
blue	bright	three	flat	loud
green	lovely	four	big	soft
orange	cute	many	huge	hard
black	adorable	few	little	tasty
white	great	some	short	sour
pink	nice	several	long	sweet

NOTE

Adjectives are also called describing words.

How Do They Compare?

ADJECTIVES THAT COMPARE

An **adjective** can be used to compare things.

Adjectives used to compare two things end with **-er**.
Adjectives used to compare three things or more end with **-est**.

This tree is the tallest of all.

This tree is taller.

This tree is tall.

This bird is small.

This bird is smaller.

This bird is the smallest of all.

Adjectives with an -er ending are often used before the word than.
Frank is *taller* **than** Jessie.

Adjectives with an -est ending are often used after the word the.
Becky is **the** *tallest* girl in our class.

The Biggest Smile

The girl has a **big** smile.
Her mother has a **bigger** smile.
The snowman has the **biggest** smile of all.

Use these special adjectives to compare.

Good				Bad		
good	better	best		bad	worse	worst

I had a **good** day.
I had a **better** day than you.
I had the **best** day of all of us.

I had a **bad** day.
I had a **worse** day than you.
I had the **worst** day of all of us.

EXTRA HELP

Here are some adjectives you can use to compare things.

funny	funnier	funniest
high	higher	highest
fast	faster	fastest
kind	kinder	kindest
easy	easier	easiest
short	shorter	shortest
few	fewer	fewest
many	more	most
little	less	least

NOTE

Before adding the **-er** or **-est** ending, you may have to double the final consonant, or change the *y* to *i*.

43

Tell More with Adverbs

ADVERBS

An adverb is a word that tells more about the verb.
Some adverbs tell **how**.

The Horse

The horse prances **gracefully**.
It gallops **fast**.

Adverbs that tell how
how the horse prances: gracefully
how the horse gallops: fast

How to Create an Adverb

Here are some adjectives that have been changed to adverbs by adding the ending **-ly**. These adverbs tell **how**.

slow	slowly
rapid	rapidly
proud	proudly
quiet	quietly
careful	carefully
swift	swiftly

44

Diving Under

Some adverbs tell when or where.

The Fish

Yesterday Carlos went diving in the sea.
He saw a beautiful fish **there**.

Adverbs that tell when and where
when Carlos went diving: yesterday
where he saw a beautiful fish: there

EXTRA HELP

Here are some adverbs you may want to use.

how	when	where
fast	now	over
sadly	today	under
beautifully	daily	here
eagerly	late	there
loudly	tomorrow	everywhere
well	suddenly	outside

NOTE

A sentence may have more than one adverb. An adverb may come before or after the verb. It may come at the beginning or end of a sentence.

45

One + One = ONE!

COMPOUND WORDS AND CONTRACTIONS

Sometimes two words are joined to make one word.

Compound words are made up of two words joined together with no letters left out. The compound word has a **new** meaning.

sail + boat = **sailboat**

A sailboat is a boat that has a sail.

rain + coat = **raincoat**

A raincoat is a coat for wearing in the rain.

foot + print = **footprint**

A footprint is a print made by a foot.

Contractions are made up of two words, too. A contraction has the **same** meaning as the two words it is formed from. When you write a contraction, you replace one or more letters with an **apostrophe**.

There aren't any sailboats on the lake.

aren't = **are not**—the apostrophe takes the place of **o**

We'll need our raincoats today.

we'll = **we will**—the apostrophe takes the place of **wi**

Let's make footprints in the sand.

let's = **let us**—the apostrophe takes the place of **u**

AT THE PARK

Here are some compound words you may want to use.

playground	sunglasses	barefoot	sandbox
football	baseball	skateboard	sidewalk
sweatshirt	headphones		popcorn

EXTRA HELP

More Contractions

I am → I'm	I will → I'll	can not → can't
he is → he's	he will → he'll	do not → don't
she is → she's	she will → she'll	does not → doesn't
it is → it's	it will → it'll	is not → isn't
we are → we're	we will → we'll	was not → wasn't
you are → you're	you will → you'll	were not → weren't
they are → they're	they will → they'll	will not → won't

Words Under Construction

PREFIXES AND SUFFIXES

Prefixes and suffixes are word parts that can be added to words. A prefix is added at the beginning of a word. A suffix is added to the ending of a word. When a prefix or suffix is added to a word, that word's meaning is changed.

Prefixes

A wonderful story begins with a puppet who comes to life. At first he was **happy**. But he got into trouble and lost his way home and so was very **unhappy**. But, the story has a **happy** ending because his father found him. This story was first **told** a long time ago. It has been **retold** many times and in many ways.

48

Suffixes

Bambi is a book about a little fawn. When Bambi and his mother go down to the meadow, they must take great **care**. They must be **careful** because sometimes **hunters** come there.

When Bambi and the other deer hear people coming to **hunt**, they make a **quick** turn and then run **quickly** into the forest where it is safe.

EXTRA HELP

The suffix *-ful* changes a word. It adds the meaning "full" to the word.

careful	colorful
tearful	beautiful
helpful	cheerful

The suffix *-ly* adds the meaning "like" to the word.

slowly	softly
nicely	quietly
evenly	happily

The suffix *-er* sometimes adds the meaning "a person who does" to a word.

singer	painter
teacher	seller
reader	pitcher

The suffix *-er* sometimes adds the meaning "more" to a word.

smaller	taller
softer	slower
faster	higher

NOTE

The word to which a prefix or suffix is added is called a **base word** or **root word**.

The Long and the Short of It

ABBREVIATIONS

An **abbreviation** is a short way of writing a word. You use abbreviations when you write dates.

DAYS	MONTHS
Sun. for Sunday	Jan. for January
Mon. for Monday	Feb. for February
Tues. for Tuesday	Mar. for March
Wed. for Wednesday	Apr. for April
Thurs. for Thursday	Aug. for August
Fri. for Friday	Sept. for September
Sat. for Saturday	Oct. for October
	Nov. for November
	Dec. for December

Because May, June, and July are such short names, they are usually not abbreviated.

You are invited to

a birthday party for

Kristen Abernathy

on Sat., Oct. 30,

from 11:00 A.M.

until 2:00 P.M.

◀····· Sat. **is short for Saturday**
Oct. **is short for October**

◀····· A.M. **means "before noon"**

◀····· P.M. **means "after noon"**

Where Kristen Lives

You use abbreviations when you write addresses.

Use these abbreviations in addresses.

Ave. for Avenue
Blvd. for Boulevard
Rd. for Road
Pl. for Place
Hwy. for Highway
Tpk. for Turnpike
S. for South
E. for East
W. for West
N. for North

N. is short for North ....
St. is short for Street ....
MN is short for Minnesota ....

Kristen Abernathy
1438 N. Adams St.
Centerville, MN 55000

EXTRA HELP

There is a two-letter abbreviation for every state and the District of Columbia.

AL Alabama	**KS** Kansas	**ND** North Dakota
AK Alaska	**KY** Kentucky	**OH** Ohio
AZ Arizona	**LA** Louisiana	**OK** Oklahoma
AR Arkansas	**ME** Maine	**OR** Oregon
CA California	**MD** Maryland	**PA** Pennsylvania
CO Colorado	**MA** Massachusetts	**RI** Rhode Island
CT Connecticut	**MI** Michigan	**SC** South Carolina
DE Delaware	**MN** Minnesota	**SD** South Dakota
DC District of Columbia	**MS** Mississippi	**TN** Tennessee
	MO Missouri	**TX** Texas
FL Florida	**MT** Montana	**UT** Utah
GA Georgia	**NE** Nebraska	**VT** Vermont
HI Hawaii	**NV** Nevada	**VA** Virginia
ID Idaho	**NH** New Hampshire	**WA** Washington
IL Illinois	**NJ** New Jersey	**WV** West Virginia
IN Indiana	**NM** New Mexico	**WI** Wisconsin
IA Iowa	**NY** New York	**WY** Wyoming
	NC North Carolina	

NOTE

Titles for people, such as **Mr.**, **Mrs.**, **Ms.**, and **Dr.** are also abbreviations. These abbreviations begin with a capital letter and end with a period. Because **Miss** is not an abbreviation, there is no period at the end.

Choose Wisely

ANTONYMS, SYNONYMS, AND HOMOPHONES

Synonyms are words that have similar meanings.

Synonyms help you use just the right word when you write. They also help you keep from using the same word over and over.

A Polish bantam is an **unusual** kind of chicken.

Its crest is like a **strange** feather hat.

I wonder if regular chickens think this chicken looks **odd**.

Unusual, strange, and **odd** are synonyms.

Antonyms are words that mean the opposite.

A chicken coop can be a very **noisy** place. Does a chicken need a **quiet** place to lay its eggs?

Noisy and **quiet** are antonyms.

Homophones are words that sound alike but are spelled differently and have different meanings. **Fowl** and **foul** are homophones.

A wild turkey is a fowl.

> This spelling is a word for "bird."

Wild turkeys take shelter when the weather is foul.

> This spelling means "unpleasant."

Both words sound alike. They rhyme with howl and owl.

Here are some other homophones.

board / bored
chews / choose
ewe / you
flea / flee
hear / here
pair / pear
peace / piece
rain / reign / rein
right / write

weak / week
for / four / fore
to / two / too
flue / flew / flu
their / there / they're
stare / stair
bare / bear
hare / hair
blue / blew

EXTRA HELP

Synonyms	Antonyms
below / under	below / above
close / shut	close / open
end / finish	end / beginning
find / locate	find / lose
hard / difficult	hard / easy
little / small	little / big
often / frequently	often / rarely
over / above	over / under
right / correct	right / wrong
start / begin	start / end

Tell, Ask, Command, Exclaim!

SENTENCES

A **sentence** is a group of words that expresses a complete thought.

At the Tennis Court
This girl is taking a tennis lesson.
What is she practicing today?

Telling Sentence:

This girl is taking a lesson.

A telling sentence tells what someone or something is or is not doing.

A telling sentence begins with a capital letter and ends with a **period**.

Question Sentence:

What is she practicing today**?**

A question sentence asks a **question**.
A question begins with a capital letter and ends with a **question mark**.
Question sentences often begin with the words **who**, **what**, **when**, **where**, **why**, or **how**.

Command Sentence:

Watch out for the ball.

A command sentence tells the listener what to do.

A command sentence begins with a capital letter and ends with a **period**.

WE WON!

The game is over now.
What a great game!

EXTRA HELP

Telling Sentence:	The star is far away.
Question Sentence:	How far away is it?
Exclamation:	How bright that star is!
Command Sentence:	Look at it now.
Telling Sentence:	The ocean is deep.
Question Sentence:	How deep is the ocean?
Exclamation:	Wow! It's so deep!
Command Sentence:	Find out how deep it is.
Telling Sentence:	They climbed a mountain.
Question Sentence:	Did they reach the top?
Exclamation:	Hooray! They finally did!
Command Sentence:	Write down their names.
Telling Sentence:	Jim ran fast.
Question Sentence:	Did he win the race?
Exclamation:	Yes! Jim won!
Command Sentence:	Give him the medal.

NOTE

A telling sentence is also called a **statement** or **declarative sentence**.

I Skate, You Skate, Everyone We Know Skates

SUBJECTS AND PREDICATES

Every sentence is made up of two parts. One part is the subject. One part is the predicate. In the examples on this page, every subject is written in blue. Every predicate is written in red.

Each word in the sentence belongs to either the **complete subject** or the **complete predicate**. The **complete subject** includes all the words that tell who or what the sentence is about. The **complete predicate** includes all the words that tell what the subject is doing.

These three children skate together in the park.

These three children is the **complete subject** of the sentence.
Skate together in the park is the **complete predicate**.

• • • • • • • • • • • •

The **simple subject** of a sentence names who or what the sentence is about.

These three children skate together in the park.

Children is the **simple subject** of the sentence.

• • • • • • • • • • • •

The **simple predicate** of a sentence tells what the subject is or what the subject does.

These three children skate together in the park.

Skate is the **simple predicate** of the sentence.

ROLLER HOCKEY

> The subject and the predicate of a sentence must agree, or be the same, in number.

If the number is one.

When the subject is **singular**, the sentence is about one person or thing. A singular subject has a singular predicate.

Dennis has skates.

In this sentence, **Dennis** is the simple subject and **has** is the simple predicate.

Dennis is singular and **has** is singular, too.

If the number is more than one.

When the subject is **plural** the sentence is about more than one person or thing. A plural subject has a plural predicate.

These kids have skates.

In this sentence, **kids** is the simple subject, and **have** is the simple predicate.

Kids is plural and **have** is plural, too.

EXTRA HELP

SINGULAR		PLURAL	
Subject	Verb	Subject	Verb
I	skate	we	skate
you	skate	you	skate
he or she	skates	they	skate
game	starts	games	start
team	plays	teams	play

NOTE

Two sentences can be joined to make one longer sentence. "Skating is fun, and hockey is fun, too." A **compound sentence** is made by joining two short, related sentences. **Sentence combining** can add variety to writing.

A Capital Idea

CAPITALIZATION

Always start with a **capital letter** when you write

- the first word in a sentence.
  (See pages 54–55 for help.)
- a proper noun.
  (See pages 30–31 for help.)
- the names of months, days, and holidays.
- the first, last, and important words in a story or book title.
  (See page 59 for help.)
- a person's title (such as *Dr., Mr.,* or *Mrs.*).
  (See pages 50–51 for help.)
- the personal pronoun *I*.

This is a street scene.

It was painted by an artist named **Jacob Kainen**.

The painting is called *The Walk*.

In the picture, **I** like the dog best.

Capitalize the first word in a sentence.

Capitalize the first letter of a person's name (a proper noun).

Capitalize the important words in titles.

Always capitalize the pronoun *I*.

In Central Park

New York **City** is the largest **city** in the United States.

It has an 840-acre **park** called Central **Park**.

People can enter from 59th **Street** and walk through the park to a **street** 50 blocks away.

There is a place in the park called the **Sheep** Meadow where **sheep** really used to graze.

Some words are capitalized when they are part of place names but not otherwise.

EXTRA HELP

Capitalization in Titles

The first and last words in a title are capitalized. So are all the important words—the nouns, pronouns, verbs, adjectives, and adverbs. The rest of the words are not capitalized. Here are some examples.

The Lion and the Mouse
Owl at Home
Make Way for Ducklings
Tales from the Jungle Book
Washday on Noah's Ark
Regards to the Man in the Moon
Cloudy with a Chance of Meatballs
On the Day You Were Born
Mitchell Is Moving
A House Is a House for Me

Always capitalize *Is*. It may not look like an important word, but it is. It's a verb.

Popular Punctuation

COMMAS

The punctuation mark that is used most is a **comma**. Commas have many different uses.

Commas in a Dialogue

When you tell what someone said, use a comma to separate **what** is said from **who** said it.

Abby said, "I love this picture!"

"Your eyes are crossed," said Luisa.

"Yeah," said Marie, "and my eyes are closed."

The comma always goes **before** the quotation marks.

This is a picture of me with two of my friends, Luisa and Abby.

> Use a comma to set off words that define, or tell about, the word that comes before it.

Luisa is smiling, and Abby has her eyes crossed.

> Use a comma to separate the two parts of a compound sentence.

Luisa, Abby, and I are best friends.

> Use commas to separate three or more nouns in a series.

Luisa and Abby are the funniest, neatest, nicest kids I know.

> Use commas to separate three or more adjectives.

They like to tell jokes, giggle, and act silly.

> Use commas to separate verbs in a series, too.

Whenever we're together, we have a great time.

> Use a comma to separate clauses in a sentence.

Dear Grandma and Grandpa,

There are many special ways to use commas when you write a letter.

April 20, 1998

Dear Grandma and Grandpa,

   We saw sharks today! It was so exciting. I never saw anything like this back home in Blaise, Indiana. The sharks swim right up to the glass. It's like you're right in the water with them. Boy, I sure wouldn't want to really be in the water with them. They are very scary.

   I wish you were here, too.

Love,
Danny

Use a comma to separate the month and day from the year.

Put a comma at the end of the greeting.

Put a comma between the city and the state.

Use a comma to set off interjections, like *Boy* or *Wow*.

Put a comma before *too* at the end of a sentence.

Put a comma after the closing.

Better Letters

CURSIVE HANDWRITING

Cursive writing has words with letters that are connected to one another. Here are some popular forms of cursive letters.

2 y's u r,
2 y's u b.
I think u r
2 y's 4 me!
Your friend,
k t

A	*a* or *a*	*N* or *N*	*n*
B or *B*	*b*	*O* or	*o* or *o*
C or *C*	*c* or *c* *c*	*P* or *P*	*p* or *p*
D or *D*	*d* or *d*	*Q* or	*q* or *q*
E or *E*	*e*	*R* or *R*	*r* or *r*
F or *F*	*f*	*S* or *S*	*s* or *s*
G or *G*	*g* or *g*	*T* or *T*	*t* or *t*
H or *H*	*h*	*U* or *U*	*u* or *u*
I or *I*	*i*	*V* or *V*	*v*
J	*j*	*W* or *W*	*w* or *w*
K or *K*	*k*	*X* or *X*	*x*
L or *L*	*l*	*Y* or *Y*	*y*
M or *M*	*m*	*Z* or *Z*	*z*

This sentence has every lowercase letter. Notice that letters slant in the same direction and spaces between words are about the same size. Your writing does not need to be perfect, but it should be easy to read.

The quick brown fox jumps over the lazy dog.

What happened here?

The quick Brown fox jumps over the lazy dog.

Handwriting Hints

Here are hints for writing cursive words so
that they are easy to read.

1. Some letters must be closed.

a   d   o   g   q   *A   D   O*

add   not *adci*   David   not *David*

log   not *lcy*   Adam   not *Adcm*

quack   not *gucick*   Ohio   not *Ohio*

2. Letters with loops should have loops, but not great big ones.

b   e   f   h   j   k   l   p   q   y   z

look   not *look*   or *look*   fuzz   not *fuzz*   or *fuzz*

ten   not *tin*   or *ten*   happy   not *happy*

3. Some letters must have dots.   *i   j*

juice   not *jiuce*   or *feece*

4. Some letters have bridges.   *b   o   v*

above   not *alcv*

5. Some letters have a cross stroke.   *t   F   H*

Hotel Fontaine   not *Hotel Fantaine*

6. Some letters go below the writing line.

f   g   j   p   q   y   z   L   2   Y   Z

foggy   not *boggy*   zoo   not *zoo*

please   not *Please*   five   not *bive*

Note: Some spelling errors are really handwriting mistakes.

Index